Understanding Rousseau

Marie-Pierre Frondziak - Laura Acquaviva

Understanding Rousseau

Max Milo

All quotations are taken from Rousseau's *Œuvres complètes* in the La Pléiade collection:

Discourse on the Sciences and Arts (Discours sur les sciences et les arts) (1st Discourse), Discourse on the Origin and Basis of Inequality Among Men (Discours sur l'origine et les fondements de l'inégalité parmi les hommes) (2d Discourse), The Social Contract (Du contrat social) (CS) in volume III, *and Emile or On Education (Émile ou De l'éducation) (E) in volume* IV.

Introduction:
Rousseau, a Revolutionary Thinker

Rousseau has often been a disparaged author. Sometimes, even today, he is not recognized as a philosopher by his peers. This ostracism is no doubt due not only to Rousseau's very special personality, but also to the often untimely nature of his work. Rousseau dabbled in everything: music, literature, theater, botany… So he didn't immediately strike us as a serious thinker, especially as he had an exacerbated sensitivity and fell out with all the recognized scholars of his time. This may well be a sign of his profound paranoia, which can nevertheless be partly explained by the fate that often befell his works. What's more, he had the audacity to go against the tide of his time: he was one of the few thinkers of his century to oppose the idea of progress, the flagship idea of the Enlightenment. And yet, not only did Rousseau leave his mark on his time, he continues to leave his mark on ours, on several levels. We know that the French revolutionaries drew a great deal of inspiration from his *Social Contract*, but we are perhaps less familiar with his thoughts on the consequences of scientific and technical progress. Some, like Yves Vargas, even see in it an early analysis of the repercussions of capitalism. Similarly, his theory of language and languages anticipates the philosophy of language of the 20th century. Last but not least, what he has to say about education has nothing to envy the pedagogues and other exponents of the educational sciences who invade us today. Rousseau is truly a precursor in many fields, and that's how we recognize great philosophers. He is the thinker of our time, and his rigorously constructed philosophy still needs to be understood and pondered.

1. A Whimsical Yet Profound Personality

Rousseau was born in Geneva in 1712. He was raised by his father, a watchmaker, his mother having died giving birth to him: "I was born crippled and ill. I cost my mother her life, and my birth was the first of my misfortunes." (*The Confessions*, L. I.) This quotation immediately highlights the way in which Rousseau will consider himself and his existence. He began his life by "killing" his mother, who and his father were a very loving couple. His father never blamed Rousseau for coming into the world, and was even tender, but Rousseau always retained a strong sense of guilt, which deeply marked his personality, and may partly explain his feeling of having always been an outsider. Indeed, Rousseau always felt himself to be a being apart, another, living and thinking different things, and having different things to say.

So Rousseau spent his time justifying his existence, first and foremost to himself. That's probably why his life was so turbulent and unstable.

In Geneva, at the age of 12, he learned his first trade: engraver. In 1728, because he returned home late and found the city gates closed, but above all because his apprenticeship master terrorized him, he left his native town for Savoie, where he met Madame de Warens, thirteen years his senior. She was to provide him with both a sentimental education and a surrogate mother, so much so that he called her "maman" (mother). They lived together episodically for a dozen years. He became very interested in music and wanted to make it his profession. He even invented a new system of musical notation without staves, which he presented to the Académie des Sciences de Paris in 1742, but which was not successful. His life was rather idle, with no real direction. He worked as a tutor in Lyon for a year (1741), then as secretary to the French ambassador in Venice for another year only (1743):

his arrogance and pretentiousness made him unbearable, and he was dismissed. Rousseau never really knew how to behave. At once modest and inflated, he was never in his rightful place, a place he would never cease to seek. In 1744, he returned to Paris and married Thérèse Levasseur, a young linen maid with whom he had five children, all of whom were abandoned to the welfare system. Voltaire (1694-1778) criticized him for this when he published *Emile or On Education*. He married Thérèse in 1768 and remained with her until her death. To justify, or at least explain, his abandonment of his children, Voltaire wrote in his *Confessions* that he wished to protect them from his in-laws, whom he considered harmful because of their poor education. He also argued that he wanted to behave like a good citizen and entrust his children to public education, following Plato's model of education in *The Republic*! Perhaps he simply felt incapable of bringing up children properly and taking responsibility for them, as he had a certain idea—even a lofty one—of what education should be, as he will tell us in *Emile*.

From 1745 to 1751, Rousseau once again earned his living as a secretary, then as a tutor, while writing short plays that failed to make him a household name. From 1749 onwards, however, Rousseau became interested in politics, and began a process of reflection that would culminate in the writing of *The Social Contract* a few years later.

Rousseau rubbed shoulders with well-known figures such as Condillac, Diderot and Hume, but eventually fell out with them, feeling ultimately misunderstood. This feeling of inadequacy made him seem like a whimsical person, always a little out of place in his social and worldly relationships, always seeming to act and think out of turn. This "inappropriate" attitude earned him mockery and hostility, which fed his feeling of being persecuted, of being the victim of a plot, and gave rise to a veritable paranoia, reinforced by his difficulty in getting his works recognized. However, Rousseau was not just a misunderstood victim; he was himself torn between two lifestyles: he wanted the recognition of the great, the worldly, while detesting and denouncing the hypocrisy of appearances. He lives

in conflict with the opposition between being and appearing. He opposed civilization, which he saw as a denaturing and perversion of man, to nature, which he saw as good and healthy. He relentlessly criticized the alteration of man as a result of his social life. What's more, he went against the grain of the dominant Enlightenment thinking of his time, and its unshakeable belief in the idea of progress. Moreover, for Rousseau, it is not understanding, or reason, that is the foremost intellectual faculty, but freedom. He was thus an intruder, an enemy, and a citizen (of Geneva), while his detractors were still only subjects. At the time, the French were still under the yoke of absolute monarchy, and Geneva was a republic. So it's not hard to see how this audacity could have aroused so much enmity...

The first of his works to achieve a certain notoriety, however, was his *Discourse on the Arts and Sciences*, for which he won a prize in the 1750 Dijon Academy competition, which asked the question: "Has the progress of science and the arts contributed to corrupting or purifying morals?" The Age of Enlightenment was profoundly confident in the idea of progress as a means of improving both man's material life and his moral behavior. In this work, however, Rousseau argues that progress, linked to social life, rather than making man and his life better, perverts them. The ease and luxury of science and the arts make people "soft", preoccupied with trivialities and oblivious to their servitude, which is then all the greater, and from which tyrants profit. To this decadent frivolity, he contrasts the natural, virile being that man was under less favorable but more humanizing conditions. So the arts and sciences do not purify morals, but on the contrary corrupt them and drive men away from virtue, if we consider that virtue consists in elevating man to humanity. This work has provoked numerous reactions, both positive and negative, and has greatly contributed to its author's reputation.

In 1752, his play *Le Devin du village (The Village Soothsayer)* was performed before Louis XV to great acclaim. But, torn as he was between his need for recognition and his rejection of courtierism, he refused to be presented to the king, which could have earned him a pension. Fiercely attached to his

independence, Rousseau continued to make a living from his work as a musical score copyist (he made transcriptions), which he had been doing since 1750.

In 1754, the Académie de Dijon put the question "What is the source of inequality among men, and whether it is authorized by natural law?" Rousseau responded, not in an attempt to win—his work deliberately exceeded the required format—but to seize the opportunity to express his political thought. Starting with an anthropological investigation, the subject of the first part, he showed that there are very few natural inequalities, but that it is the transition to society that creates these inequalities. It is the history of man and his entry into culture that will establish privileges, and give rise to the rich and the poor, the dominant and the dominated. In the second part of *Discourse on the Origin and Basis of Inequality Among Men*, Rousseau questions the legitimacy of social inequalities, showing that today's societies are the heirs to a fool's bargain that the philosopher must denounce. The aim is to show that the social order is not sacred, that it was created by man and can therefore be transformed. The end of the

Discourse heralds the theses of *The Social Contract*, namely that man, now self-aware, can free himself from his ancestral bondage. *The Discourse on the Origin and Foundations of Inequality among Men* was published in 1755. It was the subject of controversy, and was sometimes misunderstood and ridiculed, as Voltaire is reported to have said: "Il prend une envie de marcher à quatre pattes quand on lit votre ouvrage."

In *The Social Contract*, published in 1762, Rousseau set out his political theory. In effect, he was creating a treatise on political law, with the aim of determining the laws that should govern the functioning of the state, which must ensure the security of its citizens while preserving their freedom. The problem posed is to analyze the reasons why the citizens of a state must obey the laws, in other words, to ask what are the legitimate foundations of political authority. For Rousseau, who defends the idea of the republic, of public property belonging to all, the ideal regime is democracy, because this regime consists of a contract between individuals by which the people become a

people. To live with dignity, we must obey laws that the people prescribe for themselves, and not be subject to masters. When *The Social Contract* was published, it met with little success. It really came to light at the time of the French Revolution, and was particularly important for the Montagnards, including Robespierre, who called it "the gospel of the patriots". Rousseau was posthumously blamed for the Terror, since in *The Social Contract* he says that men must be "forced" to be free. Nevertheless, we must remember that, for Rousseau, authority is not found unconditionally in the people or in political power, but in conscience enlightened by reason, i.e. in educated citizens capable of following the general will.

It was in one of his last major philosophical works (1762) that Rousseau tackled the problem of education. "In the natural order, men being all equal, their common vocation is the state of man." (*E*, p. 251.) All men are therefore equal by birth, and can remain so only if they all receive an identical education. Inequality arises when there is a difference in treatment between men. Once again,

Société

Rousseau is so relevant today, when we want to introduce and, above all, formalize a multi-speed education system! If, in order to resolve inequalities, the same education must be given to all, Rousseau does not believe that it should be humanistic. In his *Discourse on the Origin and Foundations of Inequality among Men*, he already asserts that the children of his time are "spoiled" in a way, as they are not taught a taste for effort and are "spoiled", "killed indiscriminately before birth" (*2d Discourse*, p. 135). Rousseau hates books and their authors, and believes that there is no better educator than oneself. In this sense, he can be seen as a precursor of the active pedagogies that were to flourish in the 20th century with the likes of Montessori and Freinet, who advocated learning through discovery and experience. But this is not the only purpose of *Emile or On Education*. As the title suggests, the book is about education, but like its predecessors, it is also deeply political. It is the latter that we will focus on here. Indeed, the aim of education must be to form free men, and to achieve this, they must be treated from childhood as free beings.

The Social Contract and *Emile* were condemned by the Paris Parliament and banned in France, the Netherlands, Geneva and Bern.

These four works—*Discourse on the Sciences and Arts*, *Discourse on the Origin and Basis of Inequality Among Men*, *The Social Contract* and *Emile or On Education*—constitute a sustained and consistent body of thought. Rousseau begins with a diagnosis: men have been perverted by progress and social life. The explanation is the birth and development of inequality. But what man has done, he can undo: political society must be rethought and changed. For this task to be possible, we need to educate people in this sense from an early age.

Voltaire's bad jokes about Rousseau, as well as his misleading portrayal of him as a defender of the "good savage", have too often prevented us from grasping the essential philosopher in him. However, Rousseau dedicated himself to genuine philosophical reflection, in order to answer many of his questions, such as: Why can't happiness and justice be achieved? Why are men, who need each other so much, always in opposition? In this way, he left his

mark not only on revolutionaries, but also on the history of ideas, and Kant made no secret of his debt to him. Rousseau's thought, though sometimes lyrical, is rigorous, making him one of the greatest political thinkers of all time.

2. *Discourse on the Sciences and Arts (1750)*

Jean-Jacques Rousseau was a philosopher of the Age of Enlightenment, but one of the few thinkers not to have been enthusiastic about the idea of progress so widely shared by his contemporaries. In particular, he expressed his reservations about this idea in his *Discourse on the Sciences and Arts*. The speech begins abruptly and bluntly. Rousseau presents himself to the academics as an ignoramus who refuses to go along with the prevailing fashion and opinion, including that of the literati and philosophers, namely faith in the idea of progress. Rousseau is well aware that he is addressing scholars, and that he is criticizing the very thing that the development of knowledge has led to. But he justifies himself from the outset by asserting that he is only doing his duty here. Rousseau thus situates his reflection on a moral plane, a moral plane that he will never leave in his later writings. Faced with science, Rousseau chooses morality, and one could almost say man.

As Rousseau says in the preface to this opuscule, he wants to be someone who "wants to live beyond his century". Indeed, the first key idea of the first part of the *Discourse* is to assert that the more needs men create for themselves—and they create them all the more as their knowledge progresses—the more they become dependent on them, or even slaves to them, and are thus ready to accept any servitude and compromise so long as they can satisfy these needs, which we can also call desires. We can't help but think of our consumer society, which has pushed this dialectic to the extreme: creation of needs, satisfaction of those needs, creation of new needs, thanks essentially to the progress of technology, which has been able to enlist the services of science. In this sense, Rousseau was a visionary in highlighting the infernal mechanism we are experiencing today on a frightening scale.

Rousseau also attacks not only the great and the good, but also the learned, who merely accompany and encourage the "disguised" development of this servitude. Indeed, the educated pride themselves on their polite, "civilized" behavior, which they claim is the consequence of their knowledge. The more they know, the better they behave towards their fellow human beings, the more "manners" they have, but these are nothing more than manners, appearances, hypocritical attitudes that make us believe that the more knowledgeable we are, the more we respect our fellow human beings, when in reality we manipulate them even more. Rousseau criticizes them for being the vassals of the dominant, and says it with a lot of irony, but also very acerbically: "Powers of the earth, love talents, and protect those who cultivate them. Polite peoples, cultivate them: happy slaves, you owe them that delicate and fine taste you pride yourselves on; that gentleness of character and urbanity of manners which make commerce among you so binding and easy; in a word, the appearances of all the virtues without having any of them." (*1st Discourse*, p. 7.)

Rousseau hates appearances, not on principle, but because they are always false, dishonest and conceal the very inability to be a man and to behave morally: opulence, "chic", savoir-vivre go rather badly with virtue. It's all about pleasing, pretending, appearing rather than being—in short, being hypocritical. And this type of attitude gives rise to conformist behavior in order to avoid stigmatization. Instead of a society of free men, we're dealing with an undifferentiated herd of interchangeable individuals. You can no longer trust anyone, since it's impossible to know who you're dealing with as long as they fit the mold dictated by propriety. But this generalized hypocrisy doesn't make us any better; it encourages us to conceal our true thoughts, to flatter, to compare in order to discredit in a much more perfidious way, since it's under the guise of politeness. Instead of men, we're met with softened puppets who submit to their desires. All kinds of vices designed to deceive others, including oneself, are thus developed; the goal of life together being nothing more than the satisfaction of one's own self-esteem and vanity.

Rousseau doesn't confine his critique to the Enlightenment, but in his view, advances in knowledge have always gone hand in hand with increasing depravity. More precisely, advances in knowledge have always led to the depravation of our morals and the maintenance, even development, of servitude, as far back as ancient Egypt. In this sense, doesn't the increase in knowledge, and therefore ultimately the ever-greater mastery of the world and our existence, take away our fears and allow us to do what would previously have frightened us? This is undoubtedly why Rousseau "glorifies" ignorance, which spares us a certain form of denaturation, but also of decadence.

To this "rogue" man, Rousseau contrasts the boorish, unadorned but vigorous and frank man of ancient societies, who doesn't calculate because he doesn't have to try to "fool" his fellow man. Not that these simple societies were made up of stupid men, but they preferred to preserve their moral conduct and didn't sacrifice it to knowledge. They didn't put it second to elegance and refinement; they continued to value sincerity, not superficiality. We may pride ourselves on our progress and urbanity, but we are not the barbarians we think we are. To support his argument, Rousseau turns to the first of the philosophers: Socrates. Indeed, Socrates was quick to criticize the sophists (the wise men or scholars) and artists of his day, for distracting men from the search for truth, by bribing and flattering their senses. That said, Rousseau will, as he sometimes does elsewhere, twist Socrates' position a little, claiming that he too glorified ignorance, which is excessive to say the least. Socrates asserts that he knows that he doesn't know, precisely so that he can emerge from ignorance, rather than reveling in it because he confuses it with knowledge.

However, Rousseau does not idealize man before the development of civilization, stating that "human nature was basically no better" (*1st Discourse*, p. 8). However, it was simpler to understand, more "legible", which avoided the need to invent ways of deceiving others, and thus reduced the development of vices. In fact, it's not so much the sciences and arts as such that Rousseau attacks, but what we do with them. He deplores the fact that they are used for frivolity and "insulting mockery" (*1st Discourse*, p. 15). With this last expression, we can't help but think of Rousseau's bitterness in the face of his own experience, he whose gaucherie and apparent naiveté have often been mocked, as attested by Voltaire's remark on the publication of this *Discourse on the Sciences and Arts*: "Jean-Jacques is nothing but an unfortunate charlatan who, having stolen a small bottle of elixir, spilled it into a barrel of vinegar." Without realizing it, Voltaire is showing exactly what Rousseau denounces in his opuscule: the fatuity and mocking arrogance that do nothing to enhance man.

At the end of the first part of the *Discourse*, we have a first outline of the response to the Académie: progress has rather contributed to corrupting morals. But Rousseau goes on to clarify his point.

The second part begins just as brutally. The sciences and arts are born of our vices (avarice for geometry, pride for morality, etc.) and are designed to compensate for them: if we invented justice, it was to compensate for our injustices. The beginning of this section is rather surprising: the origin of science and the arts is to be found in man's original malice. Does this mean that man is not naturally good? In fact, for Rousseau, natural man, if he ever existed, is neither good nor evil; he is neutral, amoral. Natural man is a solitary being, not yet a man, but "a stupid and narrow-minded animal" (*CS*, L. I, chap. VIII, p. 364). He becomes a human being when he associates with his fellow creatures and develops distinctly human qualities (language, conscience, freedom and perfectibility). But at the same time, it develops all the human defects (injustice, avarice, greed), and it is these that give rise to the development of the sciences and the arts, whose vocation is to compensate for these initial vices. Consequently, it is not the sciences and arts that pervert men, that corrupt their morals, but it is because men are already corrupt that they are led to develop them. At the same time, they accentuate these vices, amplifying them and denaturing man even further. Rousseau therefore argues that it is better to give up the sciences and the search for truth, because they bring us less than we give them (time, effort, errors).

Rousseau goes even further: on the one hand, he weighs up all knowledge, and on the other, the time spent elaborating it—time which, in his view, is unproductive, useless to other men. Indeed, the proof is that if all this knowledge hadn't been produced, we'd be just as numerous, no more perverse, and so on. Of course, it could also be said that Rousseau is incapable of proving his point: medicine, for example, has significantly reduced mortality. He also denounces the idleness, "mother of all vices", of all those people who devote their lives to knowledge, letters and the arts in general. But isn't that what he himself does?

He also attacks luxury, which develops in tandem with the arts and sciences. Indeed, the latter encourage refinement and the display of pomp, but also wealth and the desire to enrich oneself, and inevitably always to the detriment of other men, who are then reduced to mere commodities to be monetized: "One will tell you that a man is worth in such and such a country the sum that he would be sold for in Algiers; another, following this calculation, will find countries where a man is worth nothing, and others where he is worth less than nothing. They value men like herds of cattle. According to them, a man is only worth as much to the State as he consumes in it." (*1st Discourse*, p. 20.) We can't help but note here the clear awareness of the historical and economic processes that were beginning to develop in his time, processes whose full significance can be measured today.

Idleness, luxury and wealth are opposed to virtue: how can you be fair when you want to be rich? What's more, they soften men, turning them into dilettantes and cowards who no longer have a sense of common purpose. In short, they make men selfish, preoccupied with themselves, conceited and petty.

Luxury corrupts morals, which in turn corrupts taste. Indeed, since society is nothing but trivialities, it needs trivial things. So, to please, artists will renounce their genius and produce things that are easy, but vain and quickly forgotten. Rousseau doesn't fail to take Voltaire to task here: "Tell us, famous Aroüet, how many strong male beauties you have sacrificed to our false delicacy, and how much the spirit of gallantry so fertile in little things has cost you in great ones." (*1st Discourse*, p. 21.) In passing, he also justifies his lack of notoriety, for it is undoubtedly to himself that he is thinking when he writes: "That if by chance, among men extraordinary for their talents, there is one who has firmness in the soul and refuses to lend himself to the genius of his century and debase himself by puerile productions, woe betide him! He will die destitute and forgotten". (*1st Discourse*, p. 21.)

Rousseau resented the preciousness that robbed us of strength and courage. He denounced the effeminacy of his time and contrasted it with the virility of ancient times. The more civilized men become, the softer they become, and the less vigorous and valiant they become.

If civilization weakens the body's resistance, it is also harmful to the soul. It teaches children useless things and ignores the essential. This passage is so topical that it deserves to be quoted: "Your children will be ignorant of their own language, but will speak others that are in use nowhere; they will know how to compose verses that they can barely understand: without knowing how to distinguish error from truth, they will possess the art of making them unrecognizable to others by specious arguments:

C'EST UN EUPHÉMISME ?
J'KAPTE KE DALLE À TON MESS MEC !!! LOL

but these words magnanimity, equity, temperance, humanity, courage, they will not know what they are." (*1st Discourse*, p. 24.) The sciences and arts thus contribute to inequality between men, as they value talents and despise virtues. Rousseau inveighs against the most notorious philosophers (the Stoics and Epicureans, Hobbes, Spinoza, La Mettrie): since they don't agree with each other, let them stay away from society and keep their thoughts to themselves. He even attacks the printing press, responsible for transmitting all these erroneous and corrupt ideas! Rousseau denounces impiety and the corruption of morals. Although he was not a practicing Christian, he was profoundly Christian and had no hesitation in asserting that all books should be burned! And his own? Only Bacon, Descartes and Newton find favor in his eyes, for they are geniuses who had no need of masters, and it is to them that the sciences and arts should be reserved, as surely as to himself... Rousseau justifies this by arguing that scholars should not work for their personal glory, but should put their knowledge at the service of all in order to make them better: "But as long as power alone is on one side, enlightenment and wisdom alone on another, scholars will rarely think great things, princes will more rarely do beautiful things, and peoples will continue to be vile, corrupt and unhappy." (*1st Discourse*, p. 30.)

Even if the arts and sciences have contributed to corrupting morals, this *Discourse* ends on a slightly more optimistic note: they are not to be suppressed, but they are to be put to better use.

3. *Discourse on the Origin and Foundations of Inequality among Men (1755)*

After denouncing the vanity and superficiality of the society of his day in his *Discourse on the Sciences and Arts*, which denatured man and made him evil, it was in his *Discourse on the Origin and Foundations of Inequality Among Men*, also known as the "Second Discourse", that he developed an explanation for this "decadence". To do so, he attempted a genealogy of society, developing the idea that men are naturally born equal, but that it is life in society that will be the source of inequalities between them, and therefore also the source of their conflicts. The problem posed by this second *Discourse* is therefore a political one. In his dedication to the Republic of Geneva, Rousseau sketches out the themes to be found in *The Social*

Contract. In this case, his commitment to the republic and democracy is already evident. A good and just state is one in which the people are sovereign, and where obeying the laws represents the greatest freedom, since this is tantamount to obeying oneself, and no one is above the law: "I would have liked to live and die free, that is, so subject to the laws that neither I nor anyone else could shake the honorable yoke; this salutary and gentle yoke, which the proudest heads bear all the more obediently because they are made to bear no other." (*2d Discours*, p. 112.) What a magnificent definition of the freedom that guarantees us from arbitrary domination!

Starting from the fact that natural inequalities cannot be countered, since they are a fact of nature, Rousseau turned his attention to social, institutional inequalities, i.e. those resulting from conventions decided by men. For if social inequalities (rights, functions, positions, conditions, etc.) are instituted by men, they can also be undone by them, is his key idea. These inequalities are linked to the chance of birth (and not of nature) in a society that has accumulated privileges over the centuries. However, if Rousseau shows that these inequalities are not natural, he will ask whether they can be legitimized in the name of law, or more precisely in the name of natural law, pre-existing history, which would justify a society's hierarchical construction in order to survive. The moderns, whom Rousseau criticizes, start with men "as they have made themselves" (*2d Discourse*, p. 125). They observe society, identify characteristic behaviors and can then justify property, the demand for justice and so on. However, by dissociating the natural from the acquired, Rousseau does not base positive laws on natural law (which would have men be like this or like that), and defeats conservatives whose concern is to justify the existing order. For Rousseau, law can only emerge when inequalities are already effective, and its purpose is to regulate them. So it's not natural law that authorizes inequality, which for Rousseau does not exist. It is positive law, i.e. law instituted by men, that creates and perpetuates inequalities. It is therefore possible to change things, since laws have been instituted by men. Here, he denounces a scandal: the weak have been duped. Indeed, while they believe they are protected by laws, these merely legalize violence. Thus, Rousseau categorically refuses to legitimize the ascendancy of some over others for "natural reasons", such as being physically the strongest. If some dominate others, it's by convention, agreement or fear, not by nature. It's worth noting that, at this point in the 18th century, the authority of divine right was being challenged and social inequality denounced. This explains why Rousseau's response to this question from the Académie was to reject divine right and adopt the position of natural law, which affirms the equal dignity and freedom of all men. However, this was his intended outcome, not his starting point. This is why he begins by investigating the origins of inequality, demonstrating that it is not a natural fact.

To understand why there are rich and poor, why some have power and others are dominated, etc., Rousseau builds an anthropology in the first part of the *Second Discourse*, i.e., he questions the essence of man, his *nature*, by hypothesizing that man is in a state of nature, stripped of all his social achievements. This will enable him to show that man is a denatured being, that he has distanced himself from nature by creating institutions, rules, history, etc.—what we call culture. These are the causes of inequality. Rousseau therefore begins by questioning the *origins* of these inequalities. This rationally reconstructed model of natural man—since a man in the state of nature has never been observed—will serve as the standard for his analysis of civilized man. He will show that man in the state of nature is healthy, innocent and not dominated, and bears absolutely no resemblance to civilized man: sick, unhappy and submissive.

The second part of the *Discourse* will analyze the transition from the state of nature to the political state, and the concomitant appearance of inequality. The aim is to understand the *foundations of* inequality and whether it is legitimate. Rousseau will then be able to show that inequality has its origins in history, not in nature, that it is therefore political and that it is due to human choices.

Let's take a closer look at this analysis. Rousseau's starting point is natural man. But from the outset, he warns us that he will not be writing a natural history of evolution in the manner of Buffon or Linnaeus. His aim is not to speculate on how man has evolved, but to tell us about authentic, true man. Thus, if we consider man without revealed religion and without all the achievements of generations, we find a man who lives in solitude, who is innocent, happy, independent, but rather deprived physically, compared to other animals. However, his needs are very limited and therefore easily satisfied, especially as he is stronger and more skilful than a socialized man, having only his own needs to worry about. Indeed, his natural life makes him robust, by a sort of natural necessity for survival. Rousseau also points out that, in this initial state, there are few differences between men: a physical weakness will be compensated for by a sharper mind, and so on. So, this description immediately puts forward the idea that, in the state of nature, there are virtually no inequalities. Moreover, conflict is rare, as this is a stable state devoid of passions and desires, with aggression and competition being tendencies that develop in society. Rousseau does not, however, make natural man an ideal to which we should return, as Voltaire would have us believe, for this being is also, according to Rousseau, "a stupid and narrow-minded animal" (*CS*, p. 364). So how do we explain the transition from the state of nature to the social state?

First of all, Rousseau asserts that natural man has no instincts, even if his senses are primary, insofar as he is capable of imitating all animals and taking advantage of them, which makes him superior with less effort. Rousseau's surprising assertion that man has no instincts is particularly striking, at a time when many of our contemporaries believe man to be endowed with them. Yet Rousseau is right: an instinct applies to the whole species, it's a vital need resolved in animals by nature. But while we humans obviously have vital needs, we resolve them differently depending on the culture to which we belong. In Freud's works, "*Trieb*" is sometimes translated as "instinct", whereas it's actually an impulse, which is totally different! Once again, we can note Rousseau's extremely penetrating mind. Man has no instincts, and therefore demonstrates a certain freedom. Rousseau takes the example of the pigeon and the cat: if the former is given meat and the latter fruit or seeds, they will starve to death, because nature has not programmed them to choose, but has imposed a rule from which they cannot deviate, even to survive. Conversely, man is not totally subject to nature. He can even free himself to the point of self-destruction, the height of absurdity. It is this freedom that makes *perfectibility* possible, which explains human evolution, the passage from a simple animal state to a far more sophisticated one. This disposition enables man to perfect himself, acquire new knowledge and develop his faculties, such as intelligence and reason. On an individual level, man can always improve through education, he can always learn. On a species level, history takes over, so we don't have to start all over again with every generation. Yet freedom and perfectibility are at the root of man's downfall. Indeed, thanks to his intelligence, man will develop ever more needs, which, with the emergence of consciousness, will turn into desires, which will make him unhappy because they can't always be satisfied. According to Rousseau, this transition from simple sensation to representation must have been motivated by very specific circumstances that remain unexplained. The same mystery applies to language. It must have emerged in response to a necessity for human survival. And it is with language that mankind has been able to progress, since it has enabled them to exchange and develop knowledge, but it is also with language that mankind has been able to become more opposed, to cut itself off from nature and to torment itself, since it is now aware of death. What's more, civilized man, with all his comforts, means of care and protection from predators, is far more fragile, far more deprived, despite all his inventions. Just as domesticated animals degenerate, civilized man is decadent, ever more capable of destroying himself. But at the same time, it is freedom and perfectibility that are at work in human culture and history. In this way, human history is not written "naturally", so we can already stress that inequalities are the fruit of human action, of the history we make, and not of nature.

Secondly, in order to survive, as natural conditions became more difficult, men had to associate and organize themselves to meet their needs. Unlike

Aristotle, Grotius or Locke, Rousseau believes that man is not naturally sociable. Social life, now established, has encouraged comparison between people, and developed passions, which were few and far between in the state of nature. On the other hand, the division of tasks, or social division of labor, and the establishment of hierarchies fostered differences, all the more so as some were more cunning than others: they granted themselves land, designated themselves as decision-makers, and so on. The result was dependence and domination. Against Hobbes (1588-1679), an English philosopher, Rousseau asserts that man, in the state of nature, "is [not] a wolf to man"; it is society that puts men in competition, not nature. Passions can only exist through comparison, and therefore only in social life. Comparison also requires reflection, which natural man is incapable of, since it is a faculty that develops with language. In the state of nature, man is neither good nor bad, as he is incapable of judging right and wrong. Natural man is amoral. Conversely, civilized man, because he thinks, is capable of representing and recognizing moral rules, and therefore also of evading them. It is reason that establishes the moral equality of men, but it is also reason that allows us to depart from it. Society both moralizes and depraves man. Inequalities are thus linked to the chance of birth, to the accumulation of privileges by some, and above all to the fact that it is men who make their own history, thanks to that faculty of perfectibility that enables them to evolve and is unique to them. In the state of nature, inequalities have no place, because men are alone, they don't compare themselves, they don't have passions, so they serve no purpose and that's why they don't exist. By creating institutions, and more broadly culture, men have distanced themselves from nature, thus "denaturing" them-selves, and inequalities have grown exponentially. At the same time, men have alienated themselves by submitting to other men, whose domination and wealth they legitimize by virtue of their submission. In so doing, they renounce their essential freedom. Rousseau's analysis thus led to the idea that inequa-lities are barely perceptible in the state of nature, and are therefore not natural, but the result of life in society.

If inequalities are not based on nature, how can they be legitimate? Is there a natural right that could justify the need for hierarchy in a society? In concrete terms, what happened? What is the institutionalizing event? These are the political questions that now confront Rousseau.

He sketches out the beginnings of an answer at the opening of the second part of the *Second Discourse*. It is the emergence of private property that represents the transition from the state of nature to the social state, and which is constitutive of inequality. Indeed, it determines the political order, which subsequently legitimizes de facto domination. Private property, as a founding moment, is denounced from the outset by Rousseau as a usurpation made possible, not by nature, but by language: "This is mine." (*2d Discourse*, p. 164.) In fact, property is inscribed in history, it has not always existed and will pro-voke inequality.

But let's take a closer look. Rousseau invites us into a veritable genealogy. In the early days, nature was generous and man's needs were easily met, so there was no evolution. Then obstacles appeared:

"direct" resources began to run out, and we had to protect ourselves from other species. Man therefore had to adapt, and he was able to do so thanks to the perfectibility he already possessed in terms of power. As he developed rudimentary techniques, his intelligence expanded and his consciousness emerged. He began to associate occasionally and out of interest with his fellow creatures. But the "machine" was off and running. He began to build huts, settled down and formed the first social group: the family. He had to start exchanging on a much more regular basis, and languages appeared. Thus were born the first societies. Man "tamed" himself, losing his natural character. As people came together, they were confronted with the gaze of others, and sought their recognition to ensure their existence. But this desire for recognition gave rise to competition between men. However, the desire to be recognized, i.e. to be worth more than others, is always to the detriment of others, and thus creates a scale of values, and therefore inequalities. Vanity, contempt, shame and envy were at the root of enmity between men, as well as compromise and corruption. Property then found fertile ground. The skills required for its emergence were activated: language, technology and socialization. Indeed, it presupposes a form of abstraction made possible by language: an enclosure is only a sign of ownership and can only be respected if it has been *said to be* a sign of ownership. Similarly, the enclosure is only feasible if you can make stakes. But this technical development is only possible with socialization. The same applies to agriculture: as long as I cultivate the land for my own needs, I'm not dependent on anyone and can say that the land is mine. But this "first" ownership leads to inequalities. Some will cultivate faster than others, or more, so that people will become dependent on each other, and unequal relationships will emerge, as land will be unevenly distributed. This distribution will be all the more disparate as not everyone will be a farmer: blacksmiths, masons, etc. will be needed. And so, with the social division of labor, freedom and equality will disappear. Property thus represents the founding moment of civil society, as well as that of inequality. We shouldn't have believed the impostor who "said, 'This is mine'". But once the impostor is

CECI EST
À MOI

believed, i.e. established in the opinion of others, ownership is accepted. Now, what I possess, the other does not. The more I possess, the less the other has. I want to have what the other has and I don't. The stakes should have been pulled out, because they were illegitimate. From a natural point of view, there is no justification for ownership: the land belongs to everyone.

Ownership is therefore the fruit of the organization and division of labor that lead to dependence, which in turn enables appropriation and accumulation. The economy is no longer reduced solely to the satisfaction of needs. The individual identifies with what he has, not with what he is: appearance and vanity can develop, as can comparison and rivalry between men. The result is the domination of a few over others, who are then enslaved, forcing them into poverty and violence in order to survive. A perpetual state of war began to reign, leaving the poorest and richest alike in a state of insecurity. However, it was the wealthy who were most troubled by this situation, fearing that they would be dispossessed by force. In order to protect their property, the possessors came up with "the most thoughtful project that ever entered the human mind" (*2d Discourse*, p. 177): a pact of association to ensure peace for the benefit of all. In reality, the wealthy sought only to have their right to property recognized and protected by public force, i.e. by the very people who threatened them. The trick was to get everyone interested in the project, thereby legitimizing a situation that had previously seemed illegitimate to many. Once this situation has been legitimized by law, the rich will be protected and no one will be able to challenge their rights. As we can see, this is a real fool's bargain that has confirmed a state of affairs: the domination of the rich over the poorest and the consolidation of inequalities. It is, Rousseau tells us, "reasonable to believe that a thing has been invented by those to whom it is useful rather than by those to whom it does harm" (*2d Discourse*, p. 180). It is this domination, understood as the negation of the freedom of others, that fundamentally constitutes inequality between men. But social hierarchy cannot be legitimate, because it does not originate in nature, but in historical circumstances.

This "truncated" pact was the founding act of civil society, marking the transition from the state of nature to the civil and political state. However, this ill-founded political pact made human existence unhappy. Indeed, the law is based on deception, with the many subjected to work for the benefit of the few. Instead of being an expression of the unity and freedom of the people, laws merely enshrine inequality. This is why Rousseau criticizes, among others, D'Alembert's thesis that it is the union of the weak that has produced political societies. How could the poor, who have nothing to lose but their freedom, join together to give it up? He makes the same argument against Hobbes, who maintains that men have formed societies to ensure their security, and in exchange have surrendered their freedom to the sovereign. This is the outline of the political theory that Rousseau would develop in *The Social Contract*: the state must defend the freedom of the governed, and not behave like a master imposing its own arbitrary will. It's easy to see that Rousseau is making a thinly veiled attack on absolute monarchy. However, over time, political societies have become increasingly corrupted by human self-love and ambition. Even if it means losing freedom in exchange for privileges. And the more we dominate others, the freer we believe ourselves to be, and the more we accept a system of oppression if we believe we can benefit from it. Inequality only leads to greater oppression, which in turn leads to despotism, i.e. the confiscation of power for the benefit of private interests. The result is a return to a different state of nature. The first was a state of innocence and authenticity. The second is a state of servitude and injustice, sanctioned by the law itself. We've come full circle, and we're still going around in circles. Once again, Rousseau was so clear-sighted! Today's societies are heirs to this fool's bargain. But Rousseau showed that social order is not sacred, since it is created by men. But what men have done can be undone by them, and so inequalities can be, if not abolished—which is not what Rousseau was calling for—at least greatly reduced.

Now it's time to move on to political theory, to move from fact to law, from what is to what ought to be.

4. *On The Social Contract* (1762)

Rousseau must now find a way out and a solution to the inequalities that generate domination and prevent freedom. After a first denaturation, which led us to society through a spurious contract of association, and which brought us back to a state of nature where violence and inequality reign, we need to proceed to a second denaturation and put in place a contract of government. We then move on from society to the state, not spontaneously or naturally, but by means of a contract, i.e. an *agreement*. Indeed, a contract is the mutual commitment of the two parties involved. It implies consent in exchange for an expected good. The notion of contract is a very old one, but it only concerned private individuals, and not the establishment of legitimate political power. This is why the modern era marks a turning point. Until then, and particularly in Antiquity, man was thought of only in terms of society: society was natural to man, and for Aristotle in particular, man was a political animal, i.e. an animal naturally made to live in society, and endowed with reason. Since they are endowed with reason, man's purpose is to apply to human society the same rational order that governs the order of the world. Ancient natural law thus rests on the idea of a natural finality that transcends mere individuals, and is guided by the right reason present in every man. Human society is not a product of human will, but a necessity. At the same time, from St. Paul to Bossuet, it is asserted that political authority is by divine right.

Conversely, for the contractualists, of whom Rousseau is one, the institution of society originates in the human will, and is not natural to man. The world is not the result of a universal harmony oriented by a finality, but constitutes a physical universe, based on the principle of causality. So, just as the scientific revolution, with Galileo and Newton, thought of nature in terms of its elements and explained it in terms of laws, political analysis will start from individuals, i.e. the elements, and assert that the political order is artificial, constructed. The fundamental question is: under what conditions is a political authority legitimate? Another question follows: under what conditions is it legitimate to obey a political power? It was to answer these questions that the theories of the social contract were born. In this sense, Rousseau was a man of his time. Indeed, it was in response to seventeenth-century jurists such as Grotius (*On the Law of War and Peace*, 1625) and Pufendorf (*The Law of Nature and Nations*, 1672), Dutch and German respectively, that Rousseau wrote his *Social Contract*, even if the latter also represents the solution to the problem posed in the *Second Discourse*. These contractualists, including Rousseau, share a common starting point: in the state of nature, men are independent and equal, they have the same capacities and therefore no one has a natural right to command others. They assert that the individual, as such, possesses a certain number of rights. Thus, natural law is attached to individuals, not transcending them, and concerns the individual's natural power to preserve himself.

The aim of the social contract is to guarantee this natural right. They point out that the transition from the state of nature to the civil state is based on agreements and rules, i.e., law constructed by convention, and on voluntary submission to political authority. They thus call into question the authority of divine right. However, while they freed political authority from the Church, the contractualists opposed by Rousseau conditioned the contract on a restriction of natural freedom in favor of sovereign power.

But Rousseau—and this is where his originality lies—rejects the idea that men can renounce their natural right, understood as the power to preserve themselves, in order to transfer it to a sovereign above the law, as defended by Hobbes in *Leviathan* (1651). Rousseau criticizes Hobbes for seeking to legitimize fact through law, i.e., to legitimize the already existing political order. On the contrary, Rousseau affirms the political order not as a system of domination, but as the sole guarantor of freedom understood as autonomy. However, they both take the same approach: they start from the assumption that man is in a state of nature, rather than living in society. For a contract to be possible, a "pre-contract" must have existed, i.e., a state without society. Thus, they both affirm a state of human equality in the state of nature. Their opposition stems from their interpretation of this equality, and the consequences they draw from it, in terms of the political order as it is and as it should be.

Rousseau's approach is normative, telling us what ought to be. His social contract is a kind of "refoundation". To do this, he relies on an essential idea, set out in his *Discourse on the Origin and Foundations of Inequality among Men*. This idea is that there is no such thing as natural inequality. Inequality is always a social inequality, linked to the establishment of civil status. But civil status is the result of an agreement between men. What men have done, they can undo. This is why Rousseau's social contract does not seek to legitimize the existing state of domination, as he criticizes Hobbes for doing. For him, the terrible state of nature described by Hobbes is merely a means of justifying despotism, since anything would be preferable to the Hobbesian state of nature. Already in his *Discourse on the*

Origin and Foundations of Inequality among Men, Rousseau showed that the social contract analyzed by Hobbes is a veritable fool's bargain: "Let us unite [...] to guarantee the weak from oppression, to restrain the ambitious, and to ensure to each the possession of what belongs to him. Let us institute rules of justice and peace to which all are obliged to conform [...]. In a word, instead of turning our forces against ourselves, let us gather them into a supreme power that governs us according to wise laws, that protects and defends all the members of the association [...]." (*2d Discourse,* second part, p. 177.) Indeed, Rousseau reaffirms that what is natural is possession. Ownership presupposes recognition as such. But, in his view, those who possessed imagined an agreement to guarantee their possession. By handing over all their rights to a sovereign, the possessors thereby gained the perpetuation of their possession, transformed into property and thus guaranteed by public order. It is in society that the law of the strongest reigns, and the weak have been duped: believing themselves to be protected by laws, these merely legalize violence. And so, through their poverty, they become dependent. Yet, as Rousseau points out, the reason people have given themselves leaders is to defend their freedom, not to suppress it. He denounces this legitimization of fact by law, which only benefits the most powerful, and proposes another theory of the social contract.

Despite its sometimes lyrical aspects, Rousseau's political thought is particularly rigorous and consistent.

Rousseau therefore assumes a state of nature in which men are naturally equal (same capacities, same faculties) and in which there is no evolution or progress. Moreover, in this state of nature, men are peaceful, because possession is not stable enough to drive covetousness, and needs are very limited. Furthermore, passions such as pride and self-love are not developed, as men live in isolation. So men don't have to compare or attack each other.

This is why, in a way, Rousseau refutes the idea that the foundation of political right rests on force. His analysis is as follows (*CS*, L. I, chap. III): first of all, force is not the relationship on which natural men rely; they are isolated and hardly ever in competition. Secondly, strength is a matter of fact, changeable and random: the strongest today may be the weakest tomorrow. Finally, the strongest always try to justify their power, trying to give the form of duty to their power. Thus, political power cannot be founded on strength alone. What's more, where there is submission to force, there can be no freedom. I don't obey force by choice, but by necessity. *On the other hand*, political law states what must be, and demands to be recognized. It is obeyed out of duty and obligation, and that presupposes adherence; it is not obeyed out of compulsion, which leaves us no choice. Therefore, law cannot be born of force. It's a contradiction in terms.

Similarly, political authority cannot have paternal authority as its model and foundation, as advocated by the supporters of divine right absolutism. For Rousseau, this natural authority is temporary and benevolent, lasting only as long as necessary and enduring only by agreement.

Finally, jurisconsults such as Grotius and Pufendorf asserted that political authority could be derived from the right of slavery, hence the idea of a contract as a pact of submission. For Rousseau, however, a contract implies mutual obligations, not a unilateral commitment as in the case of submission. What's more, the terms *"right"* and *"slavery"* are also antinomic.

For Rousseau, then, there can be no natural basis for political right, in the sense that it cannot be based on natural authority, whether linked to force, paternal authority or an initial condition. Right is always derived from convention: "Since no man has natural authority over his fellow man, and since force produces no right, conventions therefore remain the basis of all legitimate authority among men." (*CS*, L. i, chap. iv, p. 355.) Since natural law cannot govern the political order, the principles of political law must be derived from the civil order. Civil liberty is therefore only possible through the political order, through the pact of association, which means that each person giving himself to all gives himself to no one.

Indeed, according to Rousseau, the aim of the state is to solve the problem of the coexistence of liberties. But in the state, reciprocity between individuals is not enough: the law must apply to all. The social pact is a commitment to a whole, of which we are a part, and to all, including ourselves. This is why political order must be the result of agreement between all subjects. It is then a question of "finding a form of association which defends and protects with all the common force, the person and the goods of each associate and by which each one uniting with all nevertheless obeys only himself and remains as free as before" (*CS*, L. I, chap. VI, p. 360). Indeed: "Each one giving himself entirely, the condition is the same for all, and the condition being equal for all, no one has an interest in making it onerous for others." (*CS*, L. I, chap. VI, p. 361.) Thus, equality and reciprocity eliminate all particular and arbitrary dependence. By placing oneself at the service of all, one submits to no particular individual, and it's the same for everyone: "Everyone giving himself to all gives himself to no one." (*loc. cit.*)

In the *Second Discourse*, Rousseau had shown that man possessed two specific characteristics: perfectibility and freedom. This is why, for Rousseau, the only legitimate form of government is democracy, which affirms two principles: the sovereignty of the people and individual freedom, according to which a man cannot obey another man, but only the laws he prescribes for himself through his representatives. Thus, for Rousseau, liberty is the essential reason for the State, and equality is a condition of liberty. In this, he is opposed to Hobbes's state, which is basically based on the force and arbitrariness of the despot, who does not guarantee freedom, but rather reproduces, at least according to Rousseau, the Hobbesian state of nature.

So, renouncing an illusory unlimited freedom, or natural freedom, or independence, everyone gains an effective freedom: civil freedom, guided by reason. Although this freedom is limited, it is real, and constitutes the only possible freedom, also known as autonomy: obeying only oneself, acting in accordance with reason. For Rousseau, the social contract's guarantee of security is not enough if it is not accompanied by freedom. As he says (*CS*, L. I, chap. IV), one lives in peace even in dungeons. What's more, to renounce one's freedom, as Hobbes advocates, by handing it over to an absolute sovereign, is to renounce one's quality as a man. From this, Rousseau can draw the conclusion that to be free in the State is to obey the laws—laws laid down by the general will, in other words, to obey oneself.

But what is this general will of which Rousseau speaks? This concept has often been misunderstood. The general will is not unanimity, even if Rousseau advocates it for constitutional laws. It's not even the will of the majority. It is that which is enlightened by reason, which every reasonable will should want, it is that which wants the common good, the good of all, against all particular interests. In fact, my particular will may be in opposition to the general will: paying taxes goes against my immediate interest, and I may think that it's no big deal if I cheat. But reason can enlighten me and enable me to go beyond my particular interest and understand the general interest, which is also my longer-term interest, admittedly less immediate, but more lasting, more certain. For Rousseau, it is the people who are sovereign and who express the general will in the form of laws, in other words, who make the laws. Rousseau, if his revolutionary thinking is anything to go by, was one of the first thinkers to deny sovereignty to kings. Thus, laws are reasonable when they are valid for any reason, and they are just if they apply to everyone. Everyone must necessarily submit to the conditions they impose on others, and this is what makes fairness possible. This is the emergence of the rule of law.

The social pact is thus the guarantor of freedom, autonomy and equality, and protects us from arbitrariness. Since laws are the fruit of sovereignty, and thus of my will enlightened by reason and understood as my will, in obeying laws I am only obeying myself: "Obedience to the law we have prescribed for ourselves is freedom." (*CS*, L. I, chap. VIII, p. 365.) What better definition of freedom can there be? To voluntarily obey the laws is to be free in the State, because the will is the will of the people who pass those laws. Hence the famous expression: "There is no liberty without laws" (*Lettres écrites de la montagne [Letters Written from the Mountain]*, p. 842), civil liberty by which I mean, which does not consist in following one's whim (for example, if I stop at a red light, I may consider that my immediate liberty is hindered, or at least my desire for power, but, if I reflect a little, I can understand that the agreement made with regard to the red light protects me from chance and arbitrariness). What's more, someone who acts without law isn't really acting himself, but nature is acting in him. Likewise, anyone who acts under the law of another is a slave. Only he who acts under his own law is free.

The Rousseauist state is thus a republic, in which everyone is a stakeholder. This presupposes—and we're right in the middle of the Enlightenment—education, which makes it possible to understand that private interest necessarily depends on the common interest. Rousseau's thinking can only be understood from this premise. We can thus understand the expression "on le forcera d'être libre" (*CS*, L. I, chap. VII, p. 364), as "on veut toujours son bien, mais on ne le voit pas toujours" (*CS*, L. II, chap. III, p. 371). The search for knowledge appears as an obligation. As a human being, I owe it to myself to want to know; it's my "finality" as a human being, what gives me my dignity. Otherwise, I can only remain silent and accept. So to force a man to obey the general will is ultimately to subject him to his own reason. This is, of course, a question of political freedom. We can see this with laws and sanctions:

if I commit a criminal act, the law obliges me to assume responsibility for it, and thus to be free. In any case, justice can only function and make sense if it recognizes our freedom.

Rousseau goes even further, showing that obedience to civil laws is the key to moral freedom. Indeed, civil liberty can make man a moral being, just and master of himself, by enabling him to recognize the general interest, i.e. by being capable of thinking about the universalization of his action. For Rousseau, it is politics that determines morality, not the latter. It is therefore within civil society that human beings can develop all the faculties that make them human (reason, morality, conscience...). At the same time, this means that human beings are responsible for the society they create, which must exist solely for their own good.

The Social Contract represents the first modern theory of the foundation of the State, by asserting that civil societies originate from a contract, even if this contract as such is a fiction, and by asserting that political authority arises from a convention, and is therefore freed from divine authority. For Rousseau, it was a question of elucidating the transition to civil society, and he showed that it was common utility that ensured this transition. As men developed more and more relationships with each other, and therefore more sources of conflict, due to the development of different passions, they had to establish by convention an authority that would sort them out, in order to ensure relative peace. Moreover, it is the social pact that gives legitimacy to this authority and to the obligation to obey it. Obedience to political authority is therefore the fruit of a voluntary decision, not the result of any natural "condition". This implies that the foundation of authority lies in the individual, hence the development of individual rights and the Declaration of the Rights of Man, whose first article affirms that men are born free and equal in rights. This also means, incidentally, that the Declaration of Human Rights is based on a convention, since freedom and equality can only be guaranteed by the State. The Declaration is also largely inspired by *The Social Contract.*

Finally, with his theory of the social contract, Rousseau shows that the social contract is the work of reason, and gives us the status of worthy and free human beings. With Rousseau, however, we are dealing with what ought to be. Rousseau's thinking is normative. He can be criticized for being too abstract, for not taking sufficient account of the reality of what we are. And indeed, we have succeeded in creating democracies, but don't they resemble a sum of individuals driven by their particular interests, who come together precisely to preserve these particular interests? Of course, with democracy, the individual is recognized as a subject (in the sense of the philosophy of the subject begun with Descartes) capable of constructing the political order, since he or she is thought of as autonomous. At the same time, however, it offers the opportunity to develop individualism in the pejorative sense of the term. The state guarantees my rights, and I delegate this power to it. But in the long term, this delegation leads to a loss of interest in public affairs. And yet, the position of the individual as absolute subject is precisely what leads to the loss of autonomy: I am privately independent and publicly cared for. So, while the social contract frees us from divine or natural authority, doesn't it contain the seeds of a development of individualism that turns the desired goal on its head? So, don't we have the impression, as Rousseau himself remarked, that in the social state we are living Hobbes' state of nature, where each individual seeks to prevail over the others, solely through the use of his power? How can we explain this result? Rousseau has some-times been criticized for regarding natural man as a debonair being corrupted by life in society. But in reality, Rousseau describes natural man as neutral, neither good nor bad. Once in society, he becomes corrupted. This corruption can be explained by the various passions that animate men, but also by the specious first pact of association that made men even worse. Rousseau's desire to refound everything is a courageous one. He refuses to legitimize the existing state and proposes a new pact. One might have thought that, with the French Revolution and the establishment of the republic, this would be achieved. However, this has not been the case, and we can assume that we are now in a situation similar to that on the eve of the revolution. The political elites are no longer listening to the voters, who seem to understand nothing. If the people can't understand and accept political proposals, they are forced upon them. We can already feel the beginnings of this authoritarianism: when the people vote badly, we make them vote again. This reverses the effect and the cause, and goes completely against Rousseau: as the people vote "badly", they are prevented from voting. We need to educate the people so that they can have an informed vote, and so that they can want the general will, unless we don't want them to have an informed vote.

Rousseau had already considered the problem. The same year he published *The Social Contract*, he also published *Emile or On Education*. Once again, we can only note Rousseau's consistent thinking. Rousseau was far from naïve, and understood the need to educate citizens, to make them enlightened and therefore free, rather than slaves.

5. *Emile or On Education* (1762)

All his life, Rousseau felt remorse for abandoning his five children. *Emile or On Education* is perhaps his way of making amends.

He begins by asserting that the education given to children has always been considered bad, without anyone proposing a better one. Education, which is "the first of all utilities, which is the art of forming men, is still forgotten" (*E*, preface, p. 241). His first principle is to "consider what children are capable of learning" (*ibid.*, p. 242), not to want to see the man in the child. He thus proposes a method that does not rectify the old, but is radically new and can benefit the whole human race, no less. Plugging the "gaps" won't improve the situation.

Rousseau distinguishes two types of education: one aims to educate man and respect nature in him, as he

will do with Emile, and the other aims to make man a citizen, part of a whole at the service of the whole. The first is a domestic education to become a man, the second is a public education to fulfill oneself as a man. The latter presupposes the former. We must first learn to live, to become men: "our true study is that of the human condition" (*E*, L. I, p. 252) and "there is only one science to teach children, and that is the duties of man" (*E*, L. I, p. 266). It's all about preserving childhood, preventing denaturation from taking hold. Man must be preserved as he was born: free and equal to another man. Once again, Rousseau never separates morality and politics: we cannot live well together without having an idea of what man should be: "those who wish to treat politics and morality separately will never understand either of them" (*E*, L. IV, p. 524). An essential notion recurs regularly in Rousseau's approach to education: while we must listen to children, we must never follow their whims. Children need help to become human, but they soon realize that they can be served. With this analysis, Rousseau highlights one of the mechanisms of domination: getting children used to being at their service and making up for their weakness. The will to dominate is not inscribed in nature, but develops through the education children receive: "it does not take long experience to feel how pleasant it is to act by the hands of others, and to need only wag the tongue to make the universe move" (*E*, L. I, p. 289). Inequalities are decidedly not natural, but man-made.

In books I to III, Rousseau discusses the child's physical and intellectual development up to the age of 15. Book IV marks a turning point with puberty: "We are born, as it were, in two parts: one to exist and the other to live, one for the species, and the other for the sex." (*E*, L. IV, p. 489.) The end of book V can be seen as a summary of *The Social Contract*, which he wrote at the same time. We will therefore focus on Book IV.

Up until then, the aim had been to make a man for himself, but now the moral and social question has come to the fore, the question of how to relate to others. How can we move from individual sensitivity to social feelings and moral and political values, without denaturing man? How can sentiment and reason be (re)reconciled? How do we create a free man?

Adolescence is the moment when desire emerges, without yet being fully conscious of itself. For Rousseau, it's not a question of denying desire, but of manipulating it to direct it towards happiness and morality. It is in the natural expansion of desire, in self-love, that we find the source of moral relationships with others, just as it is in pity that we find the source of justice. As a reminder, in the *Second Discourse*, Rousseau asserted that self-love and pity are the two sentiments that pre-exist reason. Indeed, self-love is "the source of our passions, the origin and principle of all others"; it is naturally good, since it aims at the survival of the individual, and it can change into an attachment to the person who takes care of him or her, "who preserves him or her". Rousseau's fine psychological analysis can be seen here.

Mélanie Klein (an English psychoanalyst) follows a similar path to explain the emergence of moral sentiment, which arises from a feeling of gratitude towards the other, who is concerned with the preservation of our life. However, the need to be loved (to grow, to humanize oneself) is transformed into a desire to be loved. Self-love thus replaces love of

self, and all the "harmful" passions, comparisons and rivalries, can then develop. To avoid this spiral, we must conceal nothing from the almost adult, so as to avoid the work of his imagination, and regulate his feelings on the basis of his knowledge of man, so that he is not disappointed by the outside world. First of all, therefore, we need to develop pity, which can then be transformed into justice, i.e. a moral feeling, the ability to put oneself in another's place without denying one's own, without ceasing to be oneself, without envying another's place. Virtues thus have an affective foundation, not a rational one. Moral education must educate moral judgment, while not turning Emile away from men, but dissuading him from resembling them, who can "turn into ferocious beasts for not having known how to be content with being men" (*E*, L. IV, p. 532). Rousseau abhors the appearance, the semblance, the hypocrisy that social life has developed by putting an end to man's spontaneous benevolence. In the same way, self-love, transformed into self-love, must be put at the service of morality, not by taking another's place but by enhancing one's own. By making it a matter of honour to take care of the suffering and interests of others, we move from pity as a simple pursuit of individual happiness (to spare ourselves suffering) to equity and justice, to love of humankind. The contradiction between man and citizen, mentioned above, is thus on the way to being resolved. Rousseau's ethics do not rely solely on natural goodness, just as they do not transform initially immoral tendencies into virtues. Sentiment comes first, but reason and judgment are added through education. Rousseau seeks to preserve the rights of reason against superstition and mere sensation. This is why political institutions must not impose religious beliefs that are contrary to morality, and that substitute imagination for reason. This is the theme of what has come to be known as "the Savoyard vicar's profession of faith".

This can be divided into two parts. The first traces the discovery of conscience, thought of as an internal principle of unity with oneself, with reason and with others; the second examines revealed religion from the point of view of "natural religion". In this way, the vicar forces Emile to question the origin of evil and the possibility of happiness, highlighting the subject not as the source of truth, but as the source of the desire for truth, as well as the criterion of truth. The vicar was driven to question both because action poses the question of choice, notably between good and evil, and because religions impose belief even of absurdities. Rousseau thus links sentiment and reason, practice and theory: truth depends on the subject's affirmation, while at the same time imposing itself. He relies on the Cartesian subject, the universal "I" of the search for truth, while rejecting the reduction of the subject to reason and solipsistic consciousness: I cannot hope to attain truth alone. Consciousness cannot objectify itself, i.e. put itself at a distance from itself. Judgment—in this case, judgment of truth—always presupposes externalization in order to become effective; it therefore presupposes otherness, and not simply consciousness turned in on itself. What's more, it's in our relationship with nature and with others—a relationship that begins with sensation—that we reach ourselves and can hope to reach the true. By associating reason and sensation, Rousseau avoids the separation between the subject and the external object, enabling him to compare his sensations with each other and with external reality, and enabling him by analogy to understand that a will moves the body itself, just as a will moves the world, and thus to know the reality of God through this analogy. From this, Rousseau can draw the first two articles of faith of the vicar: a will moves the universe and animates nature; moreover, nature set in motion according to certain laws shows me an intelligence. Thus, nature is moved by a higher intelligence, and I can understand this idea from my own experience. Moral, biological and mechanical laws are thus on the same plane, and God is known both by his act and by his function. The divine understanding is then conceived not as the locus of eternal truths, nor merely as the condition of a general and ideal order, as revealed religions tell us, but as the act of synthesizing all reality as such. Nature dictates love of God, as the origin of all that is, and self-love (i.e. self-preservation) commands us to honor that which protects us.

Rousseau also affirms man's freedom, since he can judge his actions, not just suffer his passions, and it is this freedom that attests to conscience: "Man is therefore free of his actions, and as such animated by an immaterial substance, this is my third article of faith." (*E*, L. IV, p. 587.) This enables Rousseau to argue that it is only submission to the passions that can explain evil; only freedom can oppose it, but this freedom is not purely rational, it is also sensible. Man is therefore responsible for evil. Indeed, evil is not in the passions, but in the free submission of reason to the passions, which are the contradictions introduced into man by social and historical development and at the root of inequalities, which can also be combated thanks to the freedom of the subject, capable of judging and feeling justice, and therefore injustice. Conscience therefore stems first and foremost from the feeling of self-love and pity, which turns us towards others, and moves us from our own good to the good in general and to justice, hence the famous phrase: "Conscience! Conscience! Divine instinct, immortal and heavenly voice; sure guide of an ignorant and limited being, but intelligent and free; infallible judge of good and evil, which makes man like God, it is you who make the excellence of his nature and the morality of his actions; without you I feel nothing that raises me above the beasts, but the sad privilege of wandering from error to error with the help of an understanding without rule and a reason without principle." (*E*, L. IV, p. 600.) But the knowledge of the good presupposes reason, representation and judgment, which ensure the moral principles on which happiness is based: "The whole morality of our actions lies in the judgment we ourselves make of them." (*E*, L. IV, p. 595.)

The vicar thus affirms the autonomy of the human condition. This led him to severely criticize revealed religions, which are opposed to natural religion, and to advocate tolerance. The latter stand between man and God, developing obscure dogmas and preferring "inspiration" to argumentative debate with others, whereas reason alone is the mark of contact with truth. What's more, if we had listened only to what God says to the hearts of men, there would be only one religion. To demand the submission of reason is to outrage its author, which is why "no one is exempt from the first duty of man, no one has the right to rely on the judgment of others" (*E*, L. IV, p. 623).

The true duties of religion are independent of human institutions, and therefore of revealed religions. They are those of morality, whose first principle is inner worship, that of the heart. Rousseau's religion is thus based on freedom of conscience.

Rousseau rejects revealed religion as a source of superstition. If he defends the idea of a civil religion, it should be understood more in the sense of a morality, i.e. the rules and duties we must follow if we want to live well together. It is politics that determines morality, and Rousseau does not separate politics and morality, as we have already seen. Religious belief, understood here as the "hope of the just", sheds light on humanity's internal contradiction between nature and history, between sentiment and reason, between self-love, or personal interest, and love of humanity, or justice.

After the development of theoretical reason, Emile must gain access to reason on a practical level, in order to submit freely to reason and become autonomous, the ultimate goal of education. Rousseau attempts to reconcile reason and passion, refusing to separate them and rely on reason alone: "One of the errors of our age is to employ reason too nakedly, as if men were only spirit." (*E*, L. IV, p. 645.) But for all that, Emile makes a contract with his educator: "prevent me from being their [the passions'] slave, and force me to be my own master by not obeying my senses, but my reason" (*E*, L. IV, p. 652), a sentence that echoes that of *The Social Contract*: "To the foregoing we might add moral freedom, which alone makes man truly his own master; for the impulse of appetite alone is slavery, and obedience to the law we have prescribed for ourselves is freedom." (E, L. I, chap. VIII, p. 365.) Through this contract between Emile and his educator, Rousseau transposes natural law into moral and political law. This is why Emile ends with a "summary" of *The Social Contract*, for, after reflecting on "his moral relations with other men, it remains for him to consider himself through his civil relations with his fellow citizens" (*E*, L. V, p. 853). To do this, he must travel and reflect on the different forms of government, in order to recognize the one that suits him best.

And so we have come full circle: Rousseau has highlighted the conditions for achieving a dignified, happiness-oriented human life. Morality and politics are inseparable for the regeneration of the body politic. If, in *The Social Contract*, Rousseau makes morality dependent on politics, and in *Emile*, politics on morality, it's because both are situated in a dialectical relationship and condition each other reciprocally.

Conclusion

Rousseau, philosopher of the Enlightenment? Yes and no. No, because he rejects humanist culture and denounces the idea of progress as the source of human corruption. But yes, because his sole aim is human emancipation from all powers, whatever they may be.

Rousseau a revolutionary? Undoubtedly, even though he asserts in the *Second Discourse* that revolutions must be prevented. Robespierre, who has been blamed for so many things, not least the Terror, is said never to have gone to the Assembly without *The Social Contract* in his pocket. In many of the things the revolutionaries tried to establish, we find this desire to give the individual back his freedom, sometimes even against his will. The phrase "we'll force them to be free" may have been over-interpreted by the revolutionaries, but the fact remains that they took it from *The Social Contract.*

So, yes, Rousseau is an idealist. But he's an idealist who raises us above ourselves. It's true that freedom and obedience to reason are not naturally given to us. But it is a possibility open to us, and one that can only be achieved through education: the transmission of knowledge, the exercise of critical thinking—in other words, through the Enlightenment. To keep us in ignorance is to force us into servitude. The law of the market doesn't need us to be enlightened, it just needs us to be able to consume. For democracy to be effective, and not just a parody, real knowledge is necessary, otherwise the door is open to all possible manipulations and new barbarities.

Table of Contents